Space Disasters

Elaine Landau

*Watts* LIBRARY

Franklin Watts
A Division of Grolier Publishing
New York • London • Hong Kong • Sydney
Danbury, Connecticut

For Jayson Garmizo

Note to readers: Definitions for words in **bold** can be found in the Glossary at the back of this book.

Photographs ©: AP/Wide World Photos: 26, 50; Corbis-Bettmann: 13, 22, 23, 25, 38 (UPI); Gamma-Liaison, Inc.: 42, 44 (NASA/Paul S. Howell), cover, 3 bottom, 28, 31, 49 (NASA), 40, 47 top (USA Today); NASA: 3 top, 4, 7, 8, 10, 12, 15, 17, 33, 34, 37, 39, 47 bottom, 51; Photo Researchers: 48 (NASA/Science Source); Photri: 14; Sovfoto/Eastfoto: 20, 21 (Novosti), 18 (A. Pushkarev), 27 (TASS); Sygma: 30, 32, 35 (Tiziou).
Cover: The space shuttle *Challenger* explodes, shortly after takeoff.

Visit Franklin Watts on the Internet at:
http://publishing.grolier.com

Library of Congress Cataloging-in-Publication Data

Landau, Elaine
    Space Disasters / by Elaine Landau.
       p.   cm.— (Watts Library)
    Includes bibliographical references and index.
    Summary: Describes the accidents which occurred during the space flights of the *Apollo 1*, *Apollo 13*, and *Challenger*, as well as the Soviet space flight accidents.
      ISBN 0-531-20345-X (lib. bdg.)   0-531-16431-4 (pbk.)
    1. Space vehicle accidents—Juvenile literature. [1. Space vehicle accidents.] I. Title. II. Series.
TL867.L36 1999
363.12'4—dc21

                                              98-49176
                                              CIP
                                             AC

GROLIER
PUBLISHING

Contents

A section of the space shuttle
Challenger

A Costly Dream Come True

Have you ever dreamed of becoming an astronaut and traveling to distant parts of the universe? Just such a sense of excitement and wonder gripped the United States in the 1960s as the notion of walking on the Moon, building space stations, and visiting other planets became real possibilities. The plan behind the dream was the start of a space program in the

United States, a long-range, costly effort designed to achieve such goals.

Though it accomplished a great deal through the years, the program has not been flawless and has often been targeted by Congress for budget cuts. At times, ventures into space have also involved some degree of risk. Being an astronaut offers an opportunity for adventure and challenge, but these men and women travel to uncharted territory. In some cases, tragic accidents have cost the lives of dedicated, well-trained professionals.

This book looks at space program disasters that had especially serious consequences for those involved and the program's future goals. It is a sobering reminder that while advances are desirable, spaceflight must always be handled with caution, knowledge, and concern.

Opposite: A view of the Apollo 1 *command module after the fire*

Chapter One

Apollo 1

January 1967

It was a thrilling time for space exploration in the United States. In 1960, the Apollo space program was first introduced at a conference by the National Aeronautics and Space Administration (NASA). President John F. Kennedy was determined to see the program become a reality. Although there had been some technical and budget problems, the program aimed to put an astronaut on the Moon by 1970. The Soviet Union had launched the first manned spacecraft in 1961. Project Apollo was to take NASA to the next step—man on the Moon.

On January 27, 1967, three astronauts entered their spacecraft at John F. Kennedy Space Center in Florida for ground training. This exercise was designed to mimic the conditions of their actual spaceflight scheduled for the following month. If everything went well during the training, the trio would later enter space to determine how long and how well human beings and their equipment could function there. The information gathered would prove to be helpful in one day sending the crew to the Moon.

Apollo 1 *crew members (left to right): Edward H. White II, Virgil I. Grissom, and Roger B. Chaffee*

The *Apollo 1* Crew

The oldest of the three men was Virgil I. "Gus" Grissom, a former Air Force combat flyer. In 1966, when Grissom was

named chief pilot of the upcoming *Apollo 1* mission, the National Aeronautics and Space Administration (NASA) officials had described him as a "very astute engineer with catlike reflexes."

Roger B. Chaffee, the youngest of the group, was the only member who had never been in space before. When asked in a television interview why he became an astronaut, Chaffee replied, "The things that we'll find [in space] might give us more insight on the birth of our solar system. . . . We would be neglecting our duty . . . if we did not go."

Edward H. White II was the third member of the *Apollo 1* team. The son of a retired Army general and a graduate of West Point, White had started his career flying U.S. Army balloons, but more importantly, he was known as the first American to walk in space. White also had a reputation for being a fearless flyer. He once said, "I feel as safe in an airplane, flying around, as I do on the ground and I do feel entirely safe in a spacecraft."

The Practice Launch

During the practice exercise that January morning, the three fully suited astronauts were sealed inside their spacecraft atop a

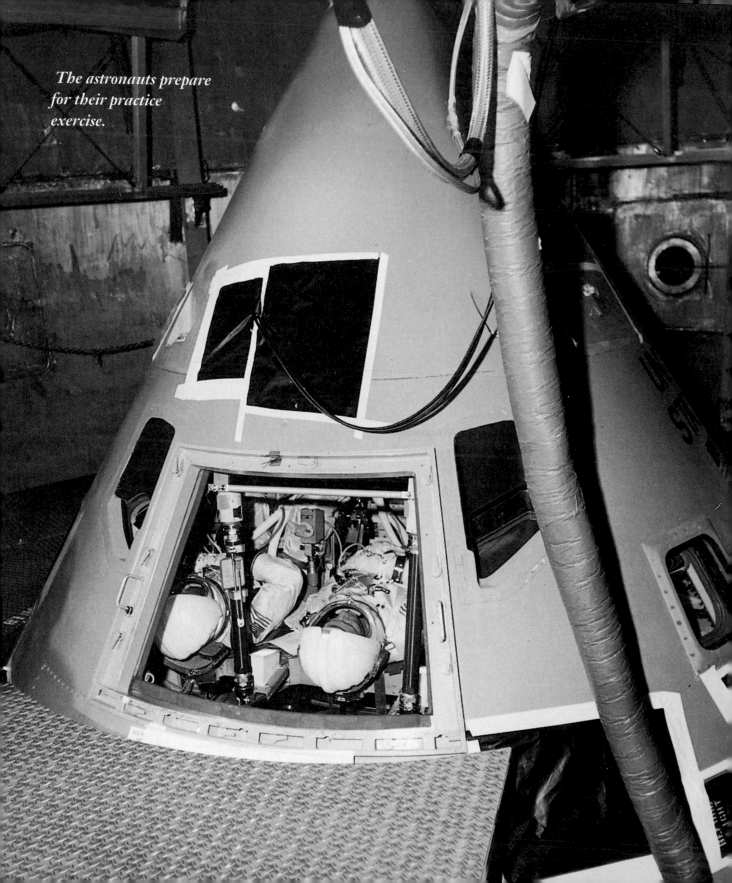

The astronauts prepare for their practice exercise.

Apollo 1's Final Moments

Recordings of the astronauts' voices to the control station, and other equipment, provide this picture of their final moments:

6:31:03 P.M.	Chaffee reports: "Fire in the spacecraft!" At that point, White's monitored heart rate shoots up significantly.
6:31:04 P.M.	There is movement by the crew within the **cockpit**, and the cabin's temperature begins to rise.
6:31:09 P.M.	White reports, "Fire in the cockpit," to the control station as the cabin pressure soars. Motion detectors indicate that movement within the cabin has increased—the astronauts are struggling to get out.
6:31:12 P.M.	Pressure in the cabin continues to rise rapidly. Chaffee indicates to the control station that the fire is extremely serious.

Communication then blurs, although some listeners think they hear "one sharp cry of pain."

Saturn 1 rocket. The team was hooked up to an environmental control system that delivered oxygen to the astronauts' suits and purified the oxygen in the cabin's air. Although pure oxygen is highly **combustible,** it had been used successfully in the past.

But NASA's luck ran out with *Apollo 1*. The astronauts had been in the spacecraft for more than five hours testing various systems when a fire broke out. Filled with highly **flammable** oxygen, the three men were doomed.

Technicians outside the spacecraft witnessed a blinding flash of light from within the capsule, followed by gusts of

heavy smoke seeping out. A group of them tried to loosen the **hatch** cover, but were driven back by the intense heat and smoke. Several of the rescue workers had to be hospitalized for smoke inhalation.

When the hatch finally sprang open, scalding air and dense clouds of smoke were released. Within the spacecraft were the charred remains of the three astronauts. Engineers estimated that the heat within the cabin must have risen "several thousand degrees," melting the astronaut's nylon spacesuits and the glass-fiber webbing on the cockpit couches. According to NASA officials, the astronauts needed ninety seconds to escape the blaze alive. "You wouldn't want a description of what we found in there," one rescue worker recalled.

A Nation Mourns

Although three other astronauts had died previously in plane crashes, the men of *Apollo 1* were the first to perish inside a spacecraft. NASA administrator James E. Webb summed up the nation's feelings when he commented, "Although everyone realized that space pilots would die, who could have thought that the first tragedy would be on the ground?"

The loss of these three outstanding astronauts sent shock waves through the nation. The public now had to acknowledge that risk was as much a part of the space program as

The command module is taken away to be studied.

13

pride and glory. The *Apollo 1* tragedy also forced NASA to reevaluate its operating policies. Chairman Clinton P. Anderson of the Senate Committee on Aeronautical and Space Sciences promised a "full review" of the circumstances leading to the three astronauts' deaths. "The use of one hundred percent oxygen in these capsules has frequently been questioned by some people in the past," he noted. "Now I think it should be questioned again."

The Use of Oxygen

Many critics opposed the use of pure oxygen in space capsules, arguing that a higher level of oxygen would burn materials a lot quicker than a lower level of oxygen. As one authority noted, "Change the **atmosphere** of a sealed chamber from a mixture of gases to pure oxygen. . . You have created a bomb, waiting only for the spark to set off the inferno."

After the *Apollo 1* disaster, NASA concluded that the use of pure oxygen during a routine exercise was hazardous. Changes were later made to *Apollo*'s system design, operations, management, and procedures to improve the safety of the spacecraft.

The practice of using oxygen in a "one gas" system had

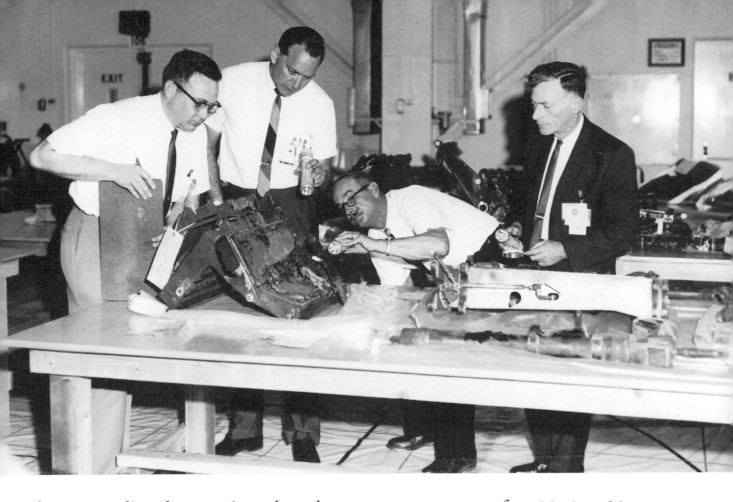

Members of the Apollo 1 Review Board Fire Panel examine a component from the spacecraft.

been appealing, because it took up less room on a spacecraft and was lighter than a less-flammable "two gas" system of oxygen and nitrogen. Although an oxygen-and-nitrogen mixture would have been similar to what we breathe on earth, it would have required more equipment to be added to the space cabin, creating extra weight. Some scientists also pointed out that with the oxygen-nitrogen system, the astronauts could die if the cabin were to suddenly **decompress**.

However, a closer look at the *Apollo 1* tragedy revealed that there were technical difficulties as well. After examining the

How Much?

The Apollo Space Program cost the U.S. government more than $23 billion. It lasted twelve years, from 1960 to 1972.

spacecraft's charred vital components, problems were found within the heating, breathing, and air-conditioning systems. Clearly, it would take many months to correct all the flaws before another trip to the Moon could be planned.

The End of Space Exploration?

The public's attitude toward the space program also began to shift following the astronauts' deaths. Many people wondered whether space exploration was really worth the cost of both human life and tax dollars. Yet those who had always supported space exploration felt certain that the program would not be abandoned as the result of financial obstacles, problems with the spacecraft's design, or even the tragic deaths of three brave and dedicated astronauts.

Chairman of the House Science and Astronautics Committee George Miller expressed his feelings about the *Apollo 1* accident: "This is a tragedy; nevertheless, it is one of the hazards that take place. Remember, every new aircraft has cost lives of test pilots, and the pilots know it. I am certain that if Grissom, White, and Chaffee could come back, they would be the first to urge that the program go on."

In the event of any technical setbacks or even their deaths, the astronauts had not wanted the Moon launch abandoned. Command pilot Grissom himself once argued the case for continuing the space program, stating, "If we die, we want people to accept it. The conquest of space is worth the risk of life."

Their dream for America's future came true on July 20, 1969, when U.S. astronaut Neil A. Armstrong took his first step on the Moon. A plaque left there read:

> HERE MEN FROM THE PLANET EARTH
> FIRST SET FOOT UPON THE MOON
> JULY 1969 A.D.
> WE CAME IN PEACE FOR ALL MANKIND

It was a day that would have made the *Apollo 1* trio proud.

A Soviet spacecraft from the early 1970s

Chapter Two

Soviet Space Disasters

In the early stages of space exploration, world powers competed against one another in what was known as "the space race." Throughout the 1960s and 1970s, the fiercest rival of the United States was the Soviet Union—a **Communist** country that has since broken up into a number of smaller nations. Both nations had invested a great deal of money, time, and effort in their space ventures. While the Soviets had many successes, they had their share of disasters as well.

"Sailors of the Stars"

The word *astronaut* was adopted by the United States after NASA began selecting and training pilots for its space projects. The Soviets called their pilots *cosmonauts,* meaning "sailors of the stars."

On April 23, 1967, only months after the *Apollo 1* disaster in the United States, a Soviet spaceship called the *Soyuz 1* exploded, killing its pilot, Vladimir M. Komarov.

Vladimir M. Komarov

Vladimir M. Komarov had always dreamed of becoming a **cosmonaut**. At the young age of fifteen, Komarov joined the Soviet Air Force. After becoming a jet fighter pilot, he earned a degree in **aeronautical** engineering to strengthen his qualifications for the space program. Although Komarov was eventually accepted as a cosmonaut, he was nearly dropped from the program when he was found to have had a heart murmur. Yet the young cosmonaut proved he was capable of space travel when he helped test the first 8-ton Soviet spacecraft, completing sixteen **orbits** around the Earth.

Vladimir M. Komarov was the first man to die during a space flight.

In 1967, Vladimir M. Komarov was given the honor of being the first Soviet to venture into space on two occasions. On this mission, he would be testing another Soviet spacecraft called the *Soyuz 1*. The first flight went well for Komarov. As he orbited the Earth, he radioed headquarters with what sounded like a prepared statement. "This [space] ship is a major creative achievement of our designers, scientists, engineers, and workers. I am proud that I was given the right to test it in flight."

Sources who were monitoring the flight from specially positioned stations, immediately recognized that Komarov had developed problems within the first twenty-four hours in space. It was clear that he would have to **abort** the mission, but when Komarov began the reentry process he was unable to fire the braking rockets.

The braking rockets slow down a spacecraft, allowing it to leave its orbit and reenter the Earth's atmosphere. Komarov had no choice but to continue orbiting the planet as he tried to manipulate the rockets. Meanwhile, his space vehicle tumbled roughly about as he sped through space.

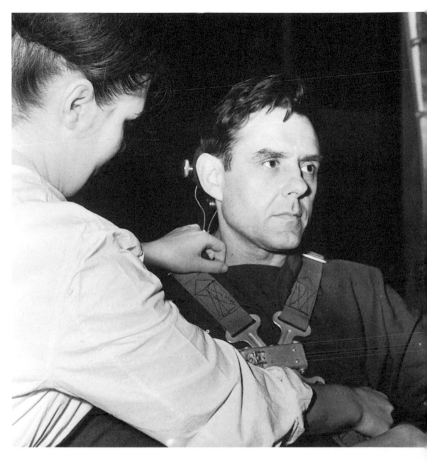

Komarov prepares for a launch exercise.

On its eighteenth orbit, the reentry rockets finally fired. For the landing to proceed smoothly, Komarov had to **deploy** the spacecraft's parachute at 23,000 feet (7,010 meters). Unfortunately, when the spacecraft was jostled and tossed in space, the parachute lines had become badly tangled. After the parachute failed to open, nothing could slow the capsule down. Soviet sources reported that Komarov died on **impact** when the space capsule struck Earth.

The Cover-Up

Although the cosmonaut's death was tragic, the Soviet government had not been honest about what had happened to the spacecraft. Critics of the space program said that the Soviet government released a story that would best protect the program. Many people believed that Komarov died before his spacecraft ever returned to Earth.

It is likely that the cabin temperature in the spacecraft began to rise rapidly when Komarov started to reenter the Earth's atmosphere. Officials stated that Komarov had made a final call to ground control—followed by silence as the spacecraft crashed hundreds of miles from its intended landing spot. Some U.S. scientists think that only one side of Komarov's spacecraft may have had a **heat shield** to protect it from the high temperature associated with reentry. Perhaps, as unprotected portions of the craft began to burn, the temperature inside the cosmonaut's cabin reached a fatal level.

Vladimir M. Komarov could not have known that this would be his last mission, but he may have had an uneasy feeling at the launch. Before stepping into the spacecraft, Komarov had

Soviet people read about Komarov's death in a Moscow newspaper.

22

Heat Shields

Heat shields are pieces of metal that were designed to protect a spacecraft from burning when reentering the Earth's atmosphere.

Upon reentering the Earth, temperatures can reach as high as 4,000 degrees Fahrenheit (2,204 Celsius).

handed a Soviet reporter a book about Joan of Arc—a historical figure who was burned at the stake. Komarov had underlined a passage that read, "She bade her farewells and continued gazing at the clear blue sky until the final second when the black smoke blotted out the sky forever."

Komarov's widow kisses a photo of her husband after his ashes have been placed in the Kremlin Wall.

First Casualty

Since manned space-flight began in 1961, Vladimir Komarov was the first space pilot to die during the course of a mission. A monument was erected near Orenburg, Russia, where Komarov's spacecraft crashed.

Some thought that Komarov's mission had been rushed so that the Soviets could boast about an impressive spaceflight accomplishment, in time for the fiftieth anniversary of their rise to power. Regardless of the circumstances surrounding his death, Vladimir M. Komarov was given the title "Hero of the Soviet Union" along with a fitting funeral. Despite hard feelings between the Soviet Union and the United States, the fallen cosmonaut was mourned internationally. U.S. president Lyndon B. Johnson stated: "The death of Vladimir M. Komarov was a tragedy in which all nations share. Like the three American astronauts who lost their lives recently, this distinguished space pioneer died in the cause of science and in the eternal spirit of human adventure."

A New Beginning

For more than a year after the crash of the *Soyuz 1*, the Soviet government refrained from launching any spacecraft. Finally, in June 1971, the Soviets launched the *Soyuz 2* carrying three cosmonauts to the *Salyut 1* **space station**, which had been established by the Soviets prior to the launch. While at the space station, the cosmonauts orbited Earth for nearly twenty-four days as they conducted scientific experiments. One of the cosmonauts, Viktor Patsayev, celebrated his thirty-eighth birthday during the mission. Millions of Soviet television viewers tuned in as Patsayev's fellow cosmonauts, Vladislav Volkov and Georgi T. Dobrovolsky, toasted him with tubes of prune paste (a type of food eaten by astronauts).

Soviet cosmonauts (from left to right) Georgi Dobrovolsky, Viktor Patsayev, and Vladislav Volkov run through a practice exercise aboard Soyuz 2.

Salyut 1 Station

On April 19, 1971, the Soviet Union sent an 18-ton space station called *Salyut 1* into space. From *Salyut 1*, cosmonauts could conduct research while in space. On June 6, 1971, *Soyuz 2* and its crew reached the space station. Vladislav Volkov and Viktor Patsayev crawled into *Salyut 1*, making it the first manned space laboratory in history.

For twenty-four days, the cosmonauts learned how to function for long periods in orbit; maneuvered and navigated the station; and conducted research in space physics, space biology, and space medicine.

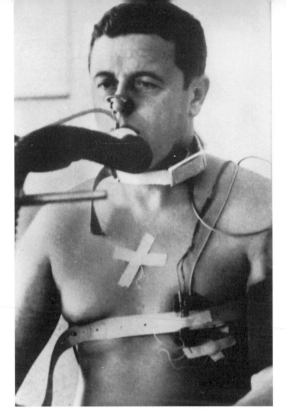

Vladislav Volkov (above) and Georgi Dobrovolsky (below) undergo medical examinations prior to their flight.

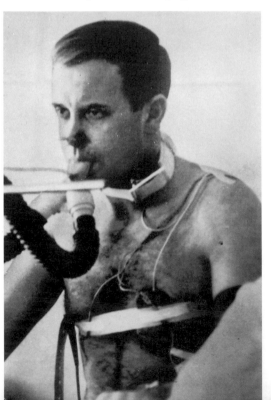

While transferring back from the space station to the attached *Soyuz 2* shuttle, mission commander Colonel Dobrovolsky reported that everything had gone smoothly. When the shuttle returned to Earth on June 29, 1971, the space recovery team opened the shuttle to help the men out, but the cosmonauts failed to respond. Seconds later, as the ground crew approached the three cosmonauts strapped in their seats, they realized that the men were dead. The tragedy shocked the Soviets. Only days before the mission was to end, physicians monitoring the cosmonauts from ground control found them in remarkably good health.

However, the mystery would end soon enough. Following an investigation into the deaths of the cosmonauts, it was determined that the men had failed to properly seal the spacecraft's hatch. As a result, their oxygen supply slipped out. The hatch opening was probably so slight that the cosmonauts never noticed it. As one reporter explained, "The *Soyuz* hatch is not unlike a car door. When the hatch is open a signal light goes on at mission control. But the light will go out when the hatch is half closed."

The Ultimate Sacrifice

Although the cosmonauts made the ultimate sacrifice, Soviet officials stressed to the public that the men had still contributed a great deal to the world's knowledge of manned space flight. Besides setting a new record for time spent in space, they had also effectively operated a complex space station. The official Soviet newspaper *Pravda* assured Soviet citizens and people throughout the world that they would not allow this tragedy to derail the space program again, noting, "We know that after this grievous loss, the difficult and dangerous struggle against nature will be continued with the same firmness and consistency. The Soviet people are used to struggle and do not retreat in the face of obstacles."

The funeral of the deceased cosmonauts

Apollo 13 is launched from Kennedy Space Center in Houston, Texas.

Chapter Three

Apollo 13

When *Apollo 13* was launched on April 11, 1970, it was to be the third time U.S. astronauts went to the Moon. *Apollo 11* had been the first to reach the Moon on July 20, 1969, and *Apollo 12* had followed in November 1969. Before *Apollo 13* launched, there were some last minute crew changes. The original *Apollo 13* crew had included its commander, Captain James A. Lovell, and astronauts Fred W. Haise, Jr., and Ken Mattingly. Only hours before the liftoff, Charles Duke, an astronaut on the *Apollo 13* backup team, came down with German measles. The three astronauts who were scheduled to go into space had been exposed to Duke. NASA officials feared that one or more of them might become ill during the mission. Testing revealed that Lovell and Haise were immune to the illness, but not Ken Mattingly.

The Decision

NASA was then faced with a difficult decision. Should they allow Mattingly to go into space and risk becoming ill on the mission or should they replace him? Symptoms of German measles, which include blurred vision and swelled joints, can be severe. If Mattingly became disabled while operating the spacecraft, there could be serious consequences. But, if the mission was postponed, the financial costs involved would be substantial.

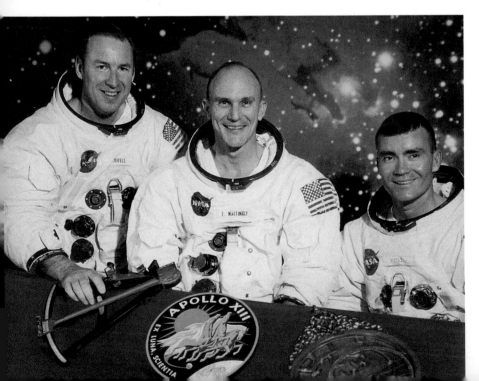

The original Apollo 13 *crew included (left to right) James A. Lovell, Ken Mattingly, and Fred W. Haise, Jr.*

One solution was to replace Mattingly with John L. Swigert, an astronaut who had also trained for the mission in case of an emergency. But while Swigert was immune to German measles, there were disadvantages to using him as a substitute. He had only trained with the *Apollo 1* backup crew and would not have much time to learn how to work closely with the other astronauts on the mission. Nevertheless, NASA officials decided to make the switch, and fortunately Swigert quickly adjusted to the crew's routine. This was especially important since Swigert would be alone in the **command module**, while Lovell and Haise were on the Moon.

John L. Swigert

If things went as planned, the results of this mission could be especially rewarding. On an earlier trip to the Moon, a Moon rock was found that was 4.5 billion years old—more than a billion years older than any rock found on Earth. Scientists hoped the *Apollo 13* astronauts would return with 5-billion-year-old rocks that dated back to the birth of the solar system.

The Modules

Apollo 13's launch went well for the first 200,000 miles (321,868 kilometers) in space. The first fifty-six hours of the flight were so routine that those at **mission control** jokingly told the astronauts, "you're putting us to sleep down here."

The *Apollo 13* craft was made up of three separate sections, or **modules.** The cone-shaped command module was

Command Module

The Apollo command module was more than 11 feet (3.3 m) high, and weighed 12,000 pounds (5,443 kg). The command module served as the flight control center and as living quarters for the crew, and was the reentry vehicle (the part that returned to Earth) at the end of the mission.

*Mission Control
communicates with
astronaut Haise (on
television screen at top).*

the space vehicle's main control area that carried the astronauts from and to the Earth. Connected to it was the service module, which held the main engine and the astronauts' oxygen, water, and fuel. The spacecraft's electrical power system was also in the service module. *Apollo 13*'s third section was its **lunar** module, the only part of the spacecraft that was to actually land on the Moon.

Shortly after 10:00 P.M. on April 13, Swigert was casually speaking to mission control in Houston when Lovell interrupted the conversation stating, "Houston, we've had a problem here." "A pretty large bang" from the service module had badly shaken the command module. As the red and yellow warning lights flashed on in the command module, the astronauts and those at Houston's mission control knew that *Apollo 13*'s flight was in trouble.

As it turned out, one of the two oxygen tanks in the service module had exploded. Looking out from his window, Lovell told mission control, "We are venting something into space. It's a gas of some sort." He was actually watching the spacecraft's oxygen supply rush out. In less than a

The Apollo 13 *service module contained a small round tank (upper left) for oxygen and a large tank (center) for hydrogen.*

33

minute, one of *Apollo 13*'s two oxygen tanks had completely emptied.

As a result of the blast, the remaining oxygen tank in the service module began to leak, and two of the three **fuel cells,** which provided most of the electrical power to the command module, were deadened.

Dr. Christopher C. Kraft, Jr.

It was obvious to the astronauts and mission control that a lunar landing was not possible. Instead, everyone began to focus on how to bring the three astronauts safely home, using the extremely limited oxygen and battery power left. With oxygen continuing to escape from the second tank, mission control knew that in less than sixty minutes, humans would not be able to survive in the command module. The only choice left was extremely risky. The astronauts would have to move into the lunar module— the small craft designed to carry only two men on the Moon for a short time.

34

In describing the danger involved, Chris Kraft, deputy director of the Manned Spacecraft Center in Houston, stated to reporters, "This is as serious a situation as we've ever had in manned spaceflight."

Coming Home

The astronauts were about 207,000 miles (333,134 km) from Earth in a spacecraft that was still rapidly approaching the Moon. Even under ideal conditions, it would take several days to bring the men home. To begin their own rescue mission, astronauts Lovell and Haise powered up the lunar module and made their way through the darkened tunnel to the module.

John Swigert stayed behind to close down the command module. He used the service module's last remnants of oxygen and power to recharge the command module's reentry batteries. This would be crucial to the astronaut's safe return. Although the lunar module could carry the men most of the way home, it lacked the necessary heat shield to withstand the extreme temperatures of reentry. Therefore, when the

This photograph of the damaged Apollo 13 *service module was taken from inside the command module while in space.*

astronauts were 30,000 miles (48,280 km) from Earth, they would have to return to the command module for their final descent. The command module had only six hours of spare power left. It was hoped that it would be enough time to allow the spacecraft to reenter the Earth's atmosphere and land.

While still in space, Lovell and Haise watched over the lunar module's vital systems as Swigert worked alone in the blackened command module. Swigert received his oxygen from a lengthy hose he had taken from Haise's space suit and connected to the lunar module. Later, two of the astronauts would take turns sleeping in the cold, unpowered command module while the third man stayed in the lunar module to ensure that all systems remained in working order.

Everyone hoped that the worst was over, but another problem threatened the astronauts' safe return. All humans inhale oxygen and exhale carbon dioxide. In space, this simple process can be life threatening, unless air purifiers remove the carbon dioxide from the air. The air purifiers in the small lunar unit were only designed to work for short periods, and they were now losing their effectiveness; so the carbon dioxide levels on board were getting dangerously high.

There were additional air purifiers in the command module, but they were not interchangeable with those in the lunar module. Therefore, to survive the astronauts had to connect a hose from the command module to their lunar "lifeboat" module. To make certain that no gas escaped, they stuffed a sock in the tube, tightening the connection.

The air-purifier box constructed by the astronauts after one of their oxygen tanks exploded

Since all the standard heating systems were shut down to conserve energy, the three men had to cope with extremely cold temperatures.

The Final Descent

Apollo 13 picked up speed as it neared Earth due to the planet's **gravitational pull**. The astronauts took their places in the command module, switched on the equipment, and sealed the hatch to prepare for their descent.

Keeping Warm

On the night before they were to return to Earth, each astronaut wore two pairs of thermal underwear to keep warm. Lovell also wore his oversized moon walking shoes to keep his toes warm.

People in New York's Grand Central Station await the outcome of Apollo 13's final descent.

As the module sped toward its final touchdown point, mission control lost all contact with the astronauts. This was the customary blackout period that occurs while a space module is surrounded by gases formed from the heat of reentry. Mission control was accustomed to reentry blackouts, but they expected the astronauts to respond to them after several minutes. When there was still no communication from the astronauts, mission control, and the millions of people around the world sitting in front of their television sets, feared the worst. Anxiously, they all waited to hear the fate of the three brave men.

Five seconds after their last call, mission control heard astronaut Swigert reply, "OK Joe." The response came exactly one-minute and forty-five seconds later than expected—making it one of the longest delays in any space mission. Nine

Anticipation

One newspaper columnist described what it was like waiting to hear from the crew of the *Apollo 13*, "I watched . . . as if by sheer will, I could mesmerize the TV reporter into telling us that all was well in the best of all possible spaceships, on the best of all possible moon probes. I couldn't and he didn't."

minutes later, the astronauts' module splashed down in the South Pacific as planned.

The medical team that was on hand to examine the astronauts found them in remarkably good condition, considering their ordeal. Meanwhile, in Houston, there was cheering and applause from mission control at the men's safe return. A few minutes later, President Nixon sent a congratulatory message to NASA on the team's miraculous rescue effort. Perhaps astronaut Swigert's father best summed up the experience: "It was a wonderful beginning and a beautiful landing, but I wouldn't give you two hoots for the interim [the time in between]."

The Apollo 13 *spacecraft is recovered after splashdown.*

Human Error

Following the near-disaster, the *Apollo 13* Review Board was assigned by NASA to investigate the incident. Officials concluded that "the explosion resulted from a highly unlikely combination of circumstances that were traceable to human oversight."

The space shuttle **Challenger** *soars into the sky.*

Chapter Four

The Challenger Flight

On January 28, 1986, Americans gathered around their TV sets and radios, and at the Cape Canaveral Air Force Base in Florida. It was to be an exciting, historic day, as the *Challenger* space shuttle was to launch into space. For twenty-five years, U.S. astronauts had journeyed into space fifty-five times, but the *Challenger* flight was considered special.

Cape Canaveral

Located on Florida's Atlantic Coast, Cape Canaveral (called Cape Kennedy from 1963 until 1973) is the major launch site for the U.S. space exploration programs. All launch operations at Cape Canaveral are conducted by NASA and the U.S. Army, Navy, and Air Force.

The *Challenger* would set a new standard for space travel since one of its crew members was not a professional astronaut. For the first time in the nation's history, an ordinary citizen would venture into space, marking the start of an era in which space travel might someday be available for everyone.

The crew was made up of both men and women with distinctly varied racial and ethnic backgrounds. The *Challenger* mission was sometimes referred to as our country's most **democratic** spaceflight. The space shuttle's crew consisted of seven individuals.

Christa McAuliffe

Christa McAuliffe, was a popular high school social studies teacher from Concord, New Hampshire. It was believed that Christa, who was loved by her students and community, would make the wonders of space a reality for the countless schoolchildren who had eagerly watched her during the preflight

training phase. Christa was to be a payload specialist aboard the *Challenger*, meaning she was on the shuttle for a one-time-only flight to carry out experiments and perform other mission-specific tasks.

At the age of thirty-seven, Christa was not only a teacher, but a wife and mother of two children, and an active community volunteer. As an able teacher, she presented material in a fascinating way, which often directly involved her students. Especially excited about her trail-blazing role on the *Challenger*, she had once remarked to her class, "When I was young, women did not fly in space."

Francis Scobee

Francis Scobee, the *Challenger*'s commanding officer, began his career in the Air Force as a mechanic when he was just eighteen years old. Attending night school and taking service education courses, Scobee earned a degree from the University of Arizona. In high school, Scobee had seemed

Opposite: The Challenger *crew (standing from left to right): Ellison Onizuka, Christa McAuliffe, Gregory Jarvis, and Judith Resnick; (sitting from left to right): Michael Smith, Francis Scobee, and Ronald E. McNair*

somewhat average. His high school football coach said, "He was never a class officer, not the star athlete, just one of the bunch." Therefore, his success in the space program was especially inspiring to those students who didn't excel academically, but still had high hopes for the future. On his last space mission, Scobee carried a banner made by the students of his former high school that read, "Trojans [the school football team] Fly High With Scobee."

Judith Resnick

Although Judith Resnick wasn't the first woman in space, her skill in math and science made her especially well qualified to be there. In high school, Resnick was the only female student in her class to receive perfect scores of eight hundred on her Scholastic Aptitude Tests (SATs).

Judith Resnick was chosen for the space program out of more than eight thousand applicants. She was to be one of the *Challenger*'s mission specialists, taking photos of Halley's comet and completing other important tasks aboard the *Challenger*.

Christa McAuliffe gets a hand from fellow astronauts during a training exercise.

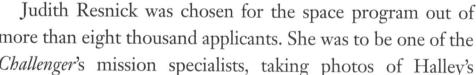

Ronald McNair

Ronald McNair, the second African-American to travel into space, had won numerous academic honors and degrees, including a Doctorate in Physics from the Massachusetts Institute of Technology (MIT). McNair would also serve as a mission specialist aboard the *Challenger*. In addressing a group of students, McNair had once said, "The true courage of space flight is not sitting aboard 6 million pounds of fire and thunder as one rockets away from this planet. True courage comes in enduring . . . persevering and believing in oneself."

Michael Smith

Michael Smith had longed to fly since he was a child. As a boy, he built an oversized wooden airplane and hung it in his yard to use as a swing. Later, he worked after school to save enough money for flying lessons. Smith flew solo in a single engine plane on his sixteenth birthday!

After graduating from the U.S. Naval Academy at Annapolis, Maryland, Smith became a Navy pilot and later entered the space program. He was one of the most experienced pilots in the astronaut corps, logging more than 4,300 hours in twenty-eight types of aircraft. He would serve as pilot aboard the *Challenger* mission.

Ellison Onizuka

Ellison Onizuka was to be the first Asian American to travel in space. While attending the University of Colorado to study **aerospace** engineering, Onizuka worked as an Air Force test pilot and flight engineer. Onizuka's primary job as a mission

Living a Dream

Following the *Challenger* disaster, Michael Smith's brother remarked, "I hope everybody realizes that Mike was doing just exactly what he wanted to do. Not many people in their lives get to do exactly what they want to do. Much less what they have wanted to do for so long."

specialist aboard the *Challenger* would be to deploy one of the largest communications **satellites** ever, the Tracking and Data Relay Satellite, designed for use by the shuttle and other spacecraft. Onizuka also trained to operate an experiment to study Halley's comet. Though he hadn't often talked about it, Onizuka had always wanted to be an astronaut. When describing her son's dreams, Onizuka's mother said, "Ellison had always had it in his mind to become an astronaut, but was too embarrassed to tell anyone. When he was growing up, there were no Asian astronauts, no black astronauts, just white ones. His dream seemed too big."

Gregory Jarvis

Early in his career, Gregory Jarvis worked as an Air Force satellite communications specialist. When he left the Air Force, he found work as a specialist in satellite systems design. On the *Challenger*, he was to conduct scientific experiments that might later lead to improved communication satellites. Jarvis wasn't afraid of space travel, noting that if anything went wrong, those at mission control "know what to do." He said he felt "excited, but not nervous," about the mission.

A Cold Morning

Despite the best hopes and dreams of everyone involved, the *Challenger* mission turned into a catastrophic disaster. When the launch took place on January 28, it had already been postponed on two prior occasions due to poor weather. At the

Challenger's final takeoff time on Tuesday, January 28, at 9:38 A.M., the crew was again presented with serious problems.

The previous day's weather forecast had called for freezing overnight temperatures, which alarmed the shuttle's **rocket booster** manufacturer. Allan J. McDonald, the engineer representing the manufacturer Morton Thiokol, Inc., strongly opposed the launching of the space shuttle that day. He and other Morton Thiokol engineers were especially concerned about the effects of extreme cold on the rocket's O-rings.

The O-rings had already caused problems in the past launch trials. At times, the tremendous pressures exerted during blastoff **dislodged** these seals. Allan McDonald was particularly uneasy about this launch, since the O-rings had never been tested at low temperatures. However, he suspected that the extreme cold would cause them to harden, shrink, and possibly open. If this occurred, the consequences would be tragic.

The seven-member crew gives a final interview before launching.

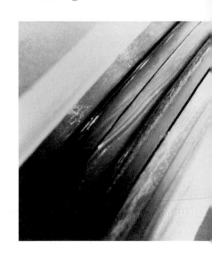

A close-up view of the O-ring that belonged to Challenger's *right solid rocket booster.*

NASA officials felt they needed to remain on schedule, and they ignored McDonald's recommendation to delay the mission. In discussions that continued throughout the evening, McDonald tried desperately to delay the launch, but he was eventually overruled. NASA had already publicly announced that there would be fifteen space shuttle flights that year, and they were determined to show both elected officials and the general public that the space program could easily reach its stated goals.

Prior to the launch of the Challenger, *ice can be seen on the launchpad.*

Count Down

On the morning of the flight, other factors indicating the mission should be canceled became evident. As early as 6:30 A.M., the temperature had fallen to a freezing 27 degrees Fahrenheit (-3 degrees Celsius), and icicles had formed on the launch pad. On three occasions, NASA sent out ice-inspection teams to evaluate the situation, but they reported that the ice did not pose a serious flight hazard. Although the inspectors didn't realize it, they were looking at something that would later prove to be crucial to the launch.

While the temperature on the left rocket booster was normal, the instruments aboard the *Challenger* indicated severe cold spots on the right booster. This meant that the booster's O-rings, which were not shielded from outside temperatures, were being subjected to much colder levels than on any flight in the past. Unfortunately, the highest NASA officials were never told about the right booster's cold spots, and the launch proceeded on schedule.

The seven astronauts boarded the shuttle that morning waving to the cheering crowd. The launch was viewed by a large group of people near the launch site and by a worldwide television audience, including many schoolchildren. The *Challenger* appeared normal as the engines were fired up, sending the shuttle soaring into the sky, high above the crowds. But, seventy-three seconds into the flight, black smoke began to spurt out from the lower portion of the shuttle's right booster rocket, an

The shuttle (top) continues flying briefly after the external tank explodes.

Rocket Boosters

A space shuttle contains two solid-fuel rocket boosters—a right and a left. Each rocket booster weighs 1,293,246 pounds (585,506 kilograms) and is 154 feet (47 meters) long.

Allan J. McDonald testifies

The Rogers Commission

Following the *Challenger* disaster, NASA conducted an extensive investigation into the causes of the disaster. It was called the Presidential Commission on the Space Shuttle *Challenger* Accident, or the Rogers Commission (after former secretary of state and chairman William P. Rogers).

Thirteen individuals (including astronauts Neil A. Armstrong and Sally Ride) sat on the commission. On June 6, 1986, the commission submitted its report to President Reagan, stating the causes of the disaster and nine recommendations for restructuring the space shuttle program, and safely returning the shuttle to flight. The redesign of the space shuttle program cost the government more then $2 billion.

area covered by an O-ring. Flames burst through the booster's casing, and within seconds, the *Challenger*'s external fuel tank exploded, turning the shuttle into a gigantic mass of fire. Crowds cried out as fragments of the *Challenger* fell into the Atlantic Ocean, 9 miles (14.5 km) above the earth. As might be expected, there were no survivors. Some experts believe that the crew members were alive and conscious during the long drop into the Atlantic. It was a day that would never be forgotten.

Shortly after the disaster, President Ronald Reagan addressed the country: "The future is not free, the story of all human progress is one of a struggle against all odds. We learned again that this America was built on heroism and noble sacrifice. It was built by men and women like our seven star voyagers who answered a call beyond duty."

Shocked by what occurred, nations throughout the world mourned the loss of the seven brave space travelers and the dream they had pursued for their country. The disaster threatened to bring the entire astronaut program to an end. For

Within a few meters from the spacecraft Discovery, *Astronaut Mark C. Lee successfully demonstrates a self-rescue device for spacewalkers.*

more than one year all shuttles were grounded while investigators studied the evidence. In the investigation following the disaster, NASA officials fared poorly. "There seems to have been a speed up policy at NASA," revealed Jerome Lederer, former director of NASA's Office of Manned Flight Safety. "There are signs of a complacency that may have set in and that's not good for safety." A NASA engineer underscored Lederer's opinion stating, "We are being driven by a launch manifest, not hardware capability or concerns about anything else."

In the years that followed the *Challenger* disaster, there were many changes at NASA. They included numerous high-level staff changes, a reevaluation of agency policy, and the introduction of new safety precautions. Eventually, the space program again became popular as the nation regained confidence in its purpose and mission. Though the *Challenger* crew will never be forgotten, others have stepped forward to finish what they began.

Timeline of Aeronautical History

1957	USSR launches the first Earth satellite, *Sputnik 1*
1958	First U.S. satellite, *Explorer 1,* is launched
1961	USSR launches the first manned spacecraft, *Vostock 1*, into orbit carrying astronaut Yuri A. Gagarin
1962	Aboard *Mercury Friendship 7*, astronaut John H. Glenn Jr. embarks on the first U.S. manned orbital flight
1964	First three-man spacecraft, *Voskhod 1*, is launched by the USSR
1965	Astronaut Edward H. White II is the first man to walk in space
1967	U.S. astronauts Virgil I. Grissom, Edward H. White II, and Roger B. Chaffee, die in a flash fire during a routine test of *Apollo 1*
1967	Vladimir M. Komarov is killed aboard *Soyuz 1*
1968	USSR launches *Zond 5*, the first unmanned, roundtrip flight to the Moon
1969	*Apollo 11* lunar-landing mission—U.S. astronauts Neil A. Armstrong and Edwin E. Aldrin Jr. are the first men to walk on the Moon
1970	U.S. astronauts James A. Lovell, Fred W. Haise, Jr., and John L. Swigert, Jr., abort their mission *Apollo 13* after an oxygen tank in the service module explodes
1971	After failing to tightly secure *Soyuz 2*'s hatch, USSR cosmonauts Georgi T. Dobrovolsky, Vladislav Volkov, and Viktor Patsayev are killed
1973	*Skylab 1*, the first U.S. space station, is placed in orbit

1975	Astronauts from an Apollo spacecraft and a Soviet Soyuz begin the first cooperative international space mission
1976	U.S. spacecraft *Viking 1* and *2* make a soft landing on Mars
1977	U.S. space shuttle makes its first test flight atop a Boeing 747 jet at Edwards Air Force Base in California
1981	U.S. space shuttle *Columbia* makes its first orbital flight with astronauts John Young and Robert Crippen
1986	Seven crew members of the space shuttle *Challenger* are killed when the shuttle's external fuel tank explodes
1988	Soviet cosmonauts Vladimir Titov and Musa Manarov set a new space-endurance record spending 365 days in orbit aboard spacecraft *Mir*
1990	U.S. space shuttle *Discovery* puts the Hubble Space Telescope into orbit around Earth
1991	U.S. space shuttle *Atlantis* puts the Compton Gamma Ray Observatory into orbit around Earth
1992	NASA begins worldwide radio telescopic search for signs of extraterrestrial life
1995	U.S. shuttle *Atlantis* docks with the Russian space station *Mir*
1997	NASA launches spacecraft *Pathfinder* to Mars
1998	American astronaut Dr. Andrew Thomas is launched into space on the *Endeavour* to join the Russian crew on the space station *Mir*
1998	After his first solo flight in 1962, astronaut John H. Glenn, Jr., returns to space aboard the space shuttle *Discovery*

Glossary

abort—to stop something from happening in the early stages

aerodynamics—a branch of science that deals with the motion of air

aeronautical—the science and practice of designing, building, and fixing aircraft

aerospace—the science of air travel and spaceflight

asphyxiation—suffocation

atmosphere—the air in a particular place

cockpit—the space or compartment from which a vehicle is steered, piloted, or driven

combustible—a substance that burns easily

command module—the area of a spacecraft that serves as the flight control center and living quarters for the crew, and is the reentry vehicle at the end of the mission

Communist—the main political party of the former Soviet Union, which practiced the principles of Communism

cosmonaut—an astronaut from the former Soviet Union or present-day Russia

decompress—to release from pressure

democratic—a political system where all people are treated fairly

deploy—to extend or spread out in width

dislodge—to force something out of position

flammable—a substance that is easily set on fire and burns rapidly

fuel cells—a device that changes the chemical energy of a fuel into an electrical energy

gravitational pull—the invisible force that pulls everything toward a planet's center

hatch—a small door or opening

heat shield—pieces of metal designed to protect a spacecraft from burning when reentering the Earth's atmosphere

impact—the forceful strike of one moving body with another

lunar—having to do with the Moon

mission control—a center that controls spaceflights

module—a self-contained unit of a spacecraft

orbit—the path followed by an object in space as it goes around another object; to travel around another object in a single path

rocket booster—a rocket that gives extra power to a spacecraft

satellite—an object that moves around a larger object

space station—a large artificial satellite designed to be occupied for long periods and to serve as a base

weightlessness—having little or no weight

To Find Out More

Books

Baird, Anne. *The U.S. Space Camp Book of Astronauts*. New York: Morrow Junior Books, 1996.

Bredeson, Carmen. *The Moon*. Danbury, CT: Franklin Watts, 1998.

Burns, Khephra. *Black Stars in Orbit: NASA's African-American Astronauts*. San Diego: Harcourt Brace & Co., 1995.

Cole, Michael D. *Apollo 13:Space Emergency*. Springfield, NJ: Enslow, 1995.

Gardner, Robert A. *Space*. New York: Twenty-First Century Books, 1994.

Kallen, Stuart A. *The Gemini Spacewalkers*. Edina, MN: Abdo & Daughters, 1996.

Kramer, Barbara. *Neil Armstrong:The First Man on the Moon*. Springfield, NJ: Enslow, 1997.

Maze, Stephanie. *I Want To Be an Astronaut*. San Diego: Harcourt Brace & Co., 1997.

Sipiera, Diane and Paul Sipiera. *Space Stations*. Danbury, CT: Children's Press, 1997.

Organizations and Online Sites

NASA Homepage
http://www.nasa.gov/
The homepage of the National Aeronautics and Space Administration, this site provides a wide variety of information for the space lover. From astronomy to space technology, this site is a must see!

The National Space Society On-Line
http://www.nss.org/
The National Space Society (NSS) focuses on technology that will one day allow people to live and work in space. Learn about the NSS society and their advances, talk to a real-life astronaut, or enter space at your own risk!

Smithsonian National Air and Space Museum
http://www.nasm.edu/
The National Air and Space Museum maintains the largest collection of aircraft and spacecraft in the world. This site allows visitors to view the collection and provides them with the historical significance of each artifact.

Starchild: A Learning Center for Young Astronomers
http://starchild.gsfc.nasa.gov/docs/StarChild/starchild.html
Learn about astronomy, space exploration, astronauts, and more at this award-winning website designed especially for youths.

Students for the Exploration and Development of Space
http://seds.lpl.arizona.edu/
Hosted by the University of Arizona, this site provides information about students' efforts to further enhance the exploration and development of astronomy, rocketry, and space science.

US Space Camp/ Aviation Challenge
http://www.spacecamp.com/
Have you ever wanted to be an astronaut or fighter pilot? Well, take the U.S. Space Camp and Aviation Challenge. Homepage of the SCAC, this site provides viewers with information on how individuals can participate in this exciting camp designed for today's youths.

A Note on Sources

In writing on space disasters, I consulted a number of resources. *The Dictionary of Space Technology*, by Mark Williamson; *Challenger: The Final Voyage*, by Richard S. Lewis; *Man Made Catastrophes*, by Lee Davis; and *The Apollo Flight That Failed*, by Henry S. F. Cooper, were all very helpful in my research.

The magazines and newspapers I consulted included *Time* magazine, *Newsweek*, *U.S. News & World Report*, and The New York *Times*. Information from NASA's Scientific and Technical Information Branch proved to be extremely useful as well.

—*Elaine Landau*

Index

Numbers in *italics* indicate illustrations.

About the Author

Popular author Elaine Landau worked as a newspaper reporter, editor, and as a youth services librarian before becoming a full-time writer. She has written more than one hundred nonfiction books for young people. Included among her many books for Franklin Watts are the other Watts Library titles on disasters: *Air Crashes*, *Fires*, and *Maritime Disasters*. Ms. Landau, who has a bachelor's degree in English and journalism from New York University and a master's degree in library and information science from Pratt Institute, lives in Miami, Florida, with her husband and son.